THE CLASSICAL GUITAR.

Selected and transcribed by
Frederick Noad.

Amsco Publications
New York/London/Sydney

Acknowledgments

I should like to express my thanks to the many librarians who have given courteous assistance during my search for early guitar editions, in particular at the British Museum, the Gesellschaft der Musikfreunde, Vienna, the Osterreichische National-Bibliothek, the Wiener Stadtbibliothek, the Bibliotheque Nationale, Paris, the Biblioteca Central and the Orfeo Catalan, Barcelona, and the Musikaliska Akademiens Biblioteket, Stockholm.

I acknowledge with gratitude the assistance of the Guitar Foundation of America and its archivist, Dr. Thomas Heck, particularly for the supply of many Giuliani original editions. Also my thanks to Ronald Purcell for the generous supply of items from his collection, and to Ako Ito and Henry Dorigny for suggesting and furnishing the original edition of their favorite Diabelli duet.

Jean Welles again helped with manuscript preparation for which I am most grateful; and no acknowledgement could sufficiently express my thanks for the constant encouragement and practical assistance of my wife Marilyn throughout this long project.

Finally I would like to express my deep appreciation to Vahdah Olcott Bickford for helpful advice and the free use of her outstanding collection.

Book design by Iris Weinstein

Illustration(s) on pages 4, 37, courtesy of the British Museum, on pages 14, 41, courtesy of the Mary Evans Picture Library, on pages 35, 105, courtesy of the Mansell Collection; on page 72, courtesy of the Library of the Royal Swedish Academy of Music; on page 74, courtesy of the Biblioteca Nacional, Madrid; on page 101, courtesy of the New York Public Library (Muller Collection).

International Standard Book Number: 0.8256.9952.5
Library of Congress Catalog Card Number: 75-16980

Distributed throughout the world by Music Sales Corporation
24 East 22nd Street, New York, NY 10010 USA
78 Newman Street, London W1P 3LA England
27 Clarendon Street, Artarmon, Sydney NSW 2064 Australia

Exclusive book trade distribution for
Alfred A. Knopf, Inc. 201 East 50th Street,
New York, NY 10022, in the United States
by Random House, Inc., New York, and
simultaneously in Canada by Random House
of Canada Limited, Toronto.

Printed in the United States of America by
Vicks Lithograph and Printing Corporation

Contents

This plate taken from Aguado's method shows a right hand position similar to that used by Spanish flamenco guitarists. A more formal position appears in Carcassi's method (see page 139).

Preface

This book represents the completion of a four year task, much of the time having been spent in locating and studying original editions or manuscripts. As a player I have been frequently irritated by the discrepancies between "revised" editions of famous guitar pieces; this research has provided the answer to many speculations about what the composers actually wrote. The editions in this book are not revised, but are reproductions of original or early publications. Fingering has been added because for every player who would like to see an unfingered *Urtext* edition, there are a hundred who expect fingering. However in many of the works, particularly Giuliani's, the fingering is implicit in the score from the form of slurring and other clues; thus the task becomes one of attempting to reveal, rather than create fingering.

The only perfect score, in fact, exists in the mind of the composer. The minute he puts pen to paper the possibility of mistake begins, and this is further compounded as the manuscript is set by the engraver; so even a first edition is subject to, and frequently contains, small errors or imperfectly expressed intentions. In an imperfect world one can only do one's best, and at least I can reassure the reader that every effort has been made to present some of the best examples of a musical period unaltered by editorial revision.

Introduction

The music in this volume is chosen from the first decades of the nineteenth century, distinguished by the term *Classical* from the Baroque guitar music of the previous two centuries and the highly romantic guitar music which was to follow.

In the early part of the previous century the guitar with its five double strings suffered a decline in popular interest, being supplanted in England by a revival of the ancient cittern, a small, wire-strung instrument sounding somewhat like a mandolin. The cittern became known as the English guitar, and sometimes simply as the guitar, which has proved a source of some confusion to historians. For instance when a niece of George Washington wrote to her uncle begging him for a guitar, the strongest possibility is that she in fact wanted a cittern.

Music for the cittern was written as for the violin, on a single staff with a treble clef, in place of the tablature systems previously associated with the plucked strings.

At the end of the century the guitar proper began to reassert its popularity, having now acquired a sixth string which increased its harmonic possibilities. In addition, single strings replaced the previous pairs, giving the appearance of greater simplicity. The music was now written as for the cittern, on a single staff, although the actual sound was an octave lower than the pitch represented. Early guitar scores also shared with the cittern a simplified approach to notation, in which the duration of separate parts was not distinguished.

instead of

To do this was, in a sense, to retain the principal disadvantage of the now defunct tablature system, and the better composers soon moved toward a reform of guitar notation establishing a style that has remained virtually unchanged to the present day.

The instrument of the period characteristically had a deeper waist than the Baroque guitar, and the number of frets was increased to as many as eighteen compared to the previous ten. In addition one may see the beginnings of a preference of rosewood for the back and sides, now considered indispensible to the concert guitar.

Perhaps the most important difference from contemporary instruments lies in the shorter string length of the early nineteenth century instrument, the closer frets permitting a greater compass of notes by the left hand. This becomes significant when the composer called for a reach which is impossible on today's guitars, necessitating in some cases a change of fingering, in others simply abandonment of the piece. Fortunately, the problem is not insuperable in the case of most composers, the major exception being Dionisio Aguado who in a large number of his works makes demands on the left hand which are quite impossible to realize on a modern fingerboard.

About The Composers

The leading figure of the period is the Catalan composer-guitarist Fernando Sor (1778-1839), whose works are more widely performed today than those of any of his contemporaries. Sor received his early musical training at the Montserrat monastery, famed for its school of sacred music, the Escolaniá, whose origin dates back to the 13th century. After leaving the monastery he composed his first opera, *Telémaco en la Isla de Calipso*, which was well received in Barcelona. In his early twenties he was accepted into the household of the Duchess of Alba, at a time when Goya was also under her patronage. In the following years he also enjoyed the favor of the powerful house of Medinaceli, from which he received both material and artistic support.

This well-connected and probably comfortable existence was to come to an end when Joseph Bonaparte was established as puppet king of Spain, and in the ensuing struggles Sor, together with other intellectuals including Goya, allied himself with the French cause. When it became apparent that, with British help, the Spanish throne would be re-established, Sor wisely emigrated to France.

This enforced exile probably did much to increase Sor's fame in the international sense. In Paris his ballet *Cendrillon* was received with considerable success, being presented no less than one hundred and four times between 1823 and 1830. His performances on the guitar prompted glowing reviews in both London and Paris, and undoubtedly were a major influence in awakening popular interest in the instrument.

His many instructional pieces show a desire to elevate the level of guitar playing, and his very interesting method was published in Spanish, French and English versions. In it he explains his ideas on technique at considerable length, including his opinion on the use of fingernails, which he regarded as an inconvenience.

The other leading figure of the period was the Italian Mauro Giuliani, whose compositions and performances earned him the respect of leading musicians of the time and who, with Sor, may be considered a prime influence in establishing a level of serious professionalism for the guitar. Whereas Sor's popularity was mainly centered in Paris and London, Giuliani reigned as the outstanding guitar virtuoso of Vienna, where he established himself in 1806 and remained until 1819. An extensive and interesting chronicle of his life there, including concert reviews, details of his association with Beethoven, Moscheles, Hummel and others is included in Thomas Heck's *The Birth of the Classic Guitar and Its Cultivation in Vienna, Reflected in the Career and Compositions of Mauro Giuliani (d. 1829)*. (Doctoral dissertation, Yale University 1970. University Microfilms, Box 1307, Ann Arbor, Michigan 48106). As a composer Giuliani was more prolific than Sor, his published compositions with opus numbers reaching 151 compared to the former's less than 70. His personality seems to have been somewhat mercurial, and having apparently saved little from his successful years he died, as did Sor, in comparative poverty.

Dionisio Aguado (1784–1849) was born in Madrid and studied the guitar under Padre Basilio (Miguel Garcia). In common with Sor and Giuliani he was interested in the reform of notation for the guitar, and in the introduction to his *Escuela de Guitarra* of 1825 cites even his own teacher as one of those who were "less fortunate in manifesting on paper that which they practised with their hands."

In 1825 Aguado visited Paris, some say expressly for the purpose of meeting Sor for whom he had considerable admiration. His modest personality seems to have endeared him to his countryman, and they became firm friends in spite of having radically different views of technique. Aguado's style involved the use of nails and scales of great speed, a type of virtuosity usually associated with the popular guitarists of Andalusia. Sor, on the other hand, seems to have been more concerned with producing a round full sound, which is consistent with the melodic quality of his compositions. In spite of these differences the two resided for a time in the same house in Paris, and for his friend and himself Sor wrote the duet *Les Deus Amis* Op. 41.

Aguado's compositions were well received in Paris, but affection for his homeland drew him back to Madrid in late 1838 where he remained until his death.

Apart from didactic works Aguado published collections of Andantes, Waltzes, Minuets etc., as well as works of a national character such as his *Fandango* Opus 16.

The Neapolitan Ferdinando Carulli (1770–1841) was essentially a self-taught guitarist who achieved celebrity as a performer. At about the age of thirty-eight he settled in Paris, where his virtuoso capacity soon won him a devoted following of students and admirers. His method became a standard work, and was followed by numerous further publications totaling eventually more than three hundred and fifty.

He was in no sense a musician of the level of Sor or Giuliani, and yet his success seems undeniable. He had the ability to write simple music within the capacity of the average amateur, and this ensured a ready reception of his work by the leading publishers.

In addition to a profusion of short solo works, Carulli wrote Sonatas for one and two guitars, numerous themes and variations, concertos with small orchestra, and a number of curious programmatic pieces interspersed with narrative text—*The Troops Begin to Embark, The Storm Rages,* and so on.

Carulli's unique position was somewhat challenged by the arrival in Paris of his younger compatriot Matteo Carcassi (1792–1853). The latter had acquired a wide reputation as a touring virtuoso, and a personal friendship with the publisher Meissonier probably helped to introduce his compositions to the Parisian public. Possessing the same gift for simplicity, Carcassi added to this a stronger melodic gift than Carulli and a more imaginative use of the higher positions of the instrument. He also favored the operatic fantasia, arrangements of popular melodies from *William Tell, Fra Diavolo* and other standards of the time.

Two guitarists of humbler abilities entered the publishing world, and both achieved considerable success. In Vienna, Anton Diabelli (1781–1858) established a position as a popular teacher of the piano and guitar, and in 1818 went into partnership with the publisher Peter Cappi to form the firm of Cappi and Diabelli. By 1824 he was in a position to buy out his partner and continue as sole proprietor. He then became Schubert's publisher, and moved in the most distinguished musical circles. Perhaps his greatest fame is derived from the thirty-three variations that Beethoven wrote on a waltz of his composition. His numerous works for solo guitar were primarily directed at amateurs, and are less interesting on the whole than the guitar duets and the small chamber works where his musical abilities are more apparent.

Antoine Meissonier (1783-18?) had already established a name as a player and teacher when in 1814 he founded the publishing company which successfully produced many guitar works including those of Carcassi. His simple compositions for solo guitar show a certain taste and elegance and are suitable for beginners.

Luigi Legnani (1790–1877) was born in Ferrara, Italy, and gained early musical experience with the opera in Ravenna. After a highly successful performance as a guitar soloist in Milan in 1819, his career was established and he toured Europe extensively. In Madrid the well-known music historian Mariano Soriano Fuertes wrote of one his concerts: "The Italian guitar virtuoso, Senor Luigi Legnani, played fantasias and brilliant variations with the full orchestra, and solos of his own composition. He displayed a most remarkable agility of execution and produced a tone of infinite depth and rare singing beauty, particularly in his cantabile on the bass strings. He was called again and again after he had already repeated his programme."

Legnani toured on a number of occasions with Paganini, playing the guitar part to the latter's duets for violin and guitar.

Giulio Regondi (1822–1872) toured Europe extensively as a child prodigy in company with a man who claimed to be his father, but who subsequently deserted him taking with him the proceeds of Regondi's successes. An article in the *Harmonicon* magazine (1831, p. 200) under the heading "Diary of a Dilettante" describes one of his London appearances: "Among the musical wonders of the day is Giulio Regondi, the child whose performances on the Spanish Guitar are not only calculated to surprise but please even connoisseurs. This most interesting prodigy, for such he may be termed, who has only reached his eighth year was born at Lyons; his mother being a native of Germany, but his father an Italian: To say that he plays with accuracy and neatness what is difficult is only doing him scanty justice; to correctness in both time and tune he adds a power of expression and a depth of feeling which would be admired in an adult; in him they show a precocity at once amazing and alarming; for how commonly are such geniuses either cut off by the preternatural action of the mind, or mentally exhausted at an age when the intellects of ordinary persons are beginning to arrive at their full strength."

In fact Regondi continued to tour successfully and to charm audiences with the particularly poetic quality of his interpretation.

Many of the celebrated Vienna composers were familiar with the guitar and played it as an accompaniment to songs. Both Schubert and von Weber were players and both published a number of songs with guitar accompaniment. In *The Guitar and Mandolin* (Schott, London. Revised edition 1954), P. J. Bone wrote, "The majority of Schubert's accompaniments were conceived on the guitar, and only afterwards did he set them for the piano, and many of his early songs were originally published with guitar. Many of his accompaniments show clearly and indisputably the influence and character of this instrument; they are in truth guitar accompaniments."

About The Music

Although the total surviving body of guitar music from the early nineteenth century is vast, yet there are few compositions that can be classified as "major works." Attempts at, for instance, sonata-allegro form are rare compared to the enormous volume of waltzes, minuets, andantes, and so on. Nevertheless the two most able composers, Sor and Giuliani, were able to approach the larger canvas and two single-movement examples are included: Sor's *Grand Solo* and Giuliani's *Grand Overture*. Both are eminently performable on the concert stage, and both use the guitar in the grand manner with orchestral suggestions in the texture.

Themes and variations were immensely popular as a form, and tended to suit the guitar because of the uniformity of key which avoided the complications of modulation to difficult positions. The variety appeared in differing rhythmic treatments, with usually a single excursion into the minor mode. Two particularly successful examples are included, Giuliani's variations on the *Harmonious Blacksmith* theme, and Sor's treatment of the ever popular *Folies d'Espagne*. For two guitars Diabelli's *Variations on a Favorite Theme* affords light-hearted entertainment of a type very characteristic of the period.

Giuliani's *Sonatina from Opus 71* is a beginner's piece, chosen in preference to many similar examples by Carulli, Carcassi and others because even within the confines of the first position the imaginativeness of the better composer is very apparent.

Arrangements of operatic themes were popular in the period, but are sparsely represented here on the assumption that a large measure of their original success was due to the fact that the tunes were already well-known which is rarely the case today.

A large body of studies have been included, not only because they provide attractive material for less advanced players, but also because the composers included some of their most charming melodies in the instructional methods that they all wrote, possibly because these methods had the potential of much wider sales than individual works or small collections.

For duet players a variety of works have been included, including a complete edition of Sor's delightful Opus 53. A very popular form of duo involved the use by the first guitar of a *capotasto* (or capodastro) clamped onto the third fret of a conventional guitar, or alternatively the use of a smaller (*Terz*) guitar tuned a minor third higher. The Diabelli duet is an example of this combination. Any prejudice that may exist against the use of this device with the classical guitar should be dispelled by the knowledge that Giuliani's nickname given to him by a frivolous secret society to which he belonged was *Vilac Umo Capodastro*.*

Ultimately, the choice of music has been based on melodic quality, since I believe that those who play the guitar are particularly concerned with melody, and a personal liking for the selected works. I realize that the collection heavily favors the work of Sor and Giuliani; but after examining literally hundreds of compositions of other composers of the period in the hope of finding a neglected masterpiece, I have come to the conclusion that there is a considerable qualitative gap between these two leading figures and all their competitors. To represent the lesser composers would have entailed robbing space from the better ones, and as this is not an historical work, the decision to emphasize Sor and Giuliani seemed unavoidable. The only significant regret I have is the inability to include good representative works of Paganini, who was a considerable guitarist as well as violinist. The only unpublished compositions that I have so far been able to acquire have not been up to the required standard, and I can only hope that in a later work I may be able to do justice to the guitar compositions of this remarkable man.

In conclusion may I wish the reader much enjoyment in exploring some of the treasures of this period.

FREDERICK NOAD

* Heck, Op. cit., Vol. I p. 117.

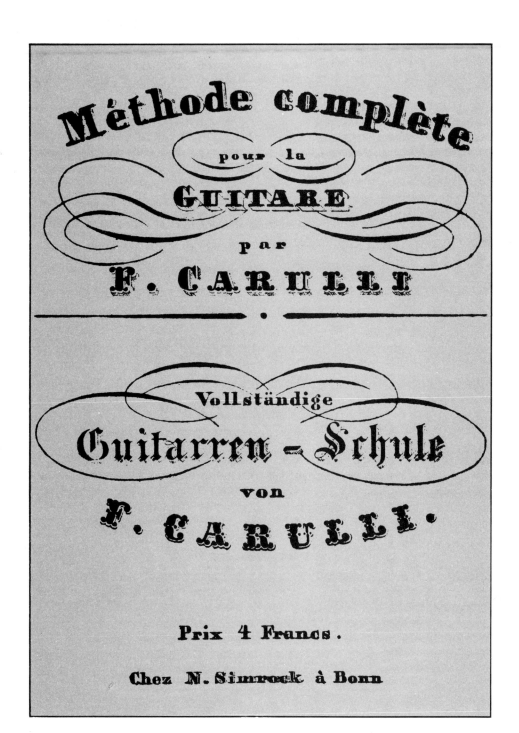

Méthode complète

pour la

GUITARE

par

F. CARULLI

Vollständige

Guitarren - Schule

von

F. CARULLI.

Prix 4 Francs.

Chez N. Simrock à Bonn

Andante

This Andante and the three pieces which follow are from Carulli's *Méthode Complète Op. 27*, composed for the instruction of his son Gustav. The popularity of these simple studies is evidenced by the continuous reprinting of them from the early nineteenth century until the present day.

1 *It is important to place the left hand 4th finger correctly on its tip to avoid touching and muting the open E string.*

Suggested tempo is ♩ = 82.

Ferdinando Carulli
(1770-1841)

Fine

Fine

D. C. al Fine

Waltz

This simple waltz is an attractive beginner's piece and should present no difficulty.
The score demonstrates early simplified notation for the classical guitar. As the form of notation developed it became customary to separate the voices with more clarity; for instance, measure three has the implication of a sustained bass note and would probably be written thus by later composers:

1 *Carulli's fingering here was:*

Suggested tempo is ♪ = 116.

Ferdinando Carulli

14

Waltz

Ferdinando Carulli

Fine

D. C. al Fine

15

Duet In G

Carulli composed this duet for student and teacher, the teacher taking the lower line. However, the lower part is only marginally more difficult than the upper, making this a simple duet for beginners.
Suggested tempo is ♩. = 76.

16

Rondo

Carulli intended this Rondo for the practise of the various left hand positions. It is not
hard to play once the fingering is understood.
For the purposes of this book it has been slightly abbreviated.
Suggested tempo is ♩ = 92.

Ferdinando Carulli

Air, Nel Cor Piu

This Aria from Paesiello's opera *La Bella Molinara* was extremely popular in the early nineteenth century, and many composers wrote instrumental variations using its tune as the theme. In his instruction method, Sor included the song as an example of style in guitar accompaniment.

The fingering is editorial, the original having none.

Guitar Arrangement
Fernando Sor

G. Paisiello
(1741-1816)

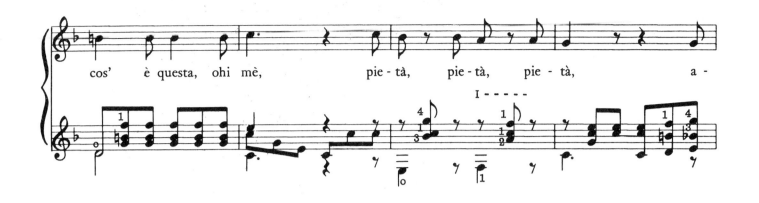

cos' è questa, ohi mè, pie - tà, pie - tà, pie - tà, a -

mo - re è un-cer - to che che de - li - rar mi fà.

Four Easy Studies

In 1820 Aguado published a series of ambitious studies for the guitar, which apparently were considered too difficult for most players. As a result, Aguado set about preparing a method (*Escuela de Guitarra*) that would include graduated lessons to lead up to the execution of his advanced studies.

The method was published in 1825, and contained many delightful easier "lessons". Those included here are numbers 48, 70, 80 and 94 from the 1825 edition. Fingering has been added to clarify Aguado's somewhat sparse indications.

No. 1 In C

1 *Care should be taken to make this progression of chords as smooth as possible in spite of the necessary jumps of the left hand.*

Suggested tempo is ♩ = 72.

Dionisio Aguado
(1784-1849)

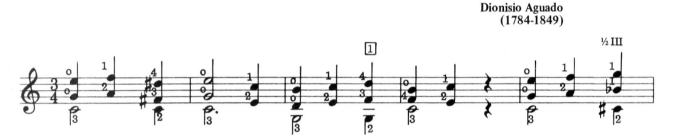

22

No. 2 In E

Aguado writes of this study that the melody part will be played by the middle and ring fingers (m) and (a), the lower parts by the thumb and index fingers (p) and (i).

[1] *The cross fingering enables the second finger to remain on the E in preparation for the following chord.*

Suggested tempo is ♪ = 88.

No. 3 In A

Aguado's note to this study indicates that it should be played as if in three voices because of the tied notes. He also points out that in order to hold the tied notes for their full value, the usual order of the left hand fingering has to be modified to prepare for the notes immediately following. This becomes apparent after playing the piece.
Suggested tempo is ♪ = 132.

No. 4 In E

In his instructions for this study Aguado recommends concentrating the attention on the longer notes in each chord, i.e., the part which sustains.
Suggested tempo is ♩ = 52.

Sonatine

Op. 71 No. 1

This work was composed "for the use of beginners" and demonstrates Giuliani's capacity to create music within the confines of the first and second positions. There are few extended works for beginning players, and the Sonatine serves a useful purpose in this respect. The fingering is editorial.

1. *To ensure a smooth transition to the F major chord which follows, the full bar should be placed in advance of the C.*
2. *Note the use of the first finger on the A to release the second finger for the bass B which follows.*
3. *It is necessary to accent the initial B of this measure to show that it is a new phrase rather than the end of the previous one; otherwise, the piece will sound as if it is a measure short.*

Sonatine
Op. 71 No. 1

Mauro Giuliani
(1781-1829)

28

Trio

D. C. Menuetto
sino al Fine

Rondo
Allegretto

Andante

Antoine Meissonier, a native of Marseilles, became attracted to the guitar when on a business trip to Naples as a young man. He eventually abandoned his business career in favor of the guitar, and moved to Paris where he enjoyed considerable success as a player, teacher, and later as a music publisher. He wrote a number of simple pieces which show charm and harmonic variety, as for example, this Andante printed in Hamilton's *Spanish Guitar Tutor*, an early nineteenth century method. The fingering is editorial.
Suggested tempo ♩ = 40.

A. Meissonier
(1783-18?)

Cradle Song (Wiegenlied)

Op. 13 No. 2

This lullaby is an example of one of the many songs written originally with guitar accompaniment by celebrated composers of the early nineteenth century which have been largely ignored by music historians and even excluded by a strange prejudice from so-called complete editions. The gentle nature of the song makes it far more suitable for accompaniment with the guitar than the pianoforte as substituted in later transcriptions.

C. M. von Weber
(1786-1826)
Words by von Hiemer

Schlaf Her - zen Söhn - chen mein Leib - ling bist du. Schlies - se die

blau - en Guck _ au - ge - lein _ zu. Al - les ist ru - hig ist

still wie im _ Grab, Schlaf nur ich weh - re die _ Flie - gen dir _ ab.

Carl Maria von Weber

Jezt noch mein Püppchen ist goldene Zeit
Später, ach später ists nimmer wie heut.
Stellen einst Sorgen ums Lager sich her,
Herzchen da schläft sich's so ruhig nicht mehr.

Engel vom Himmel so lieblich wie du,
Schweben ums Bettchen und lächeln dir zu.
Später zwar steigen sie auch noch herab
Aber sie wischen nur Thränen dir ab.

Schlafe lieb's Söhnchen und kommt gleich die Nacht,
Sitzt deine Mutter am Bettchen und wacht.
Sey es so spät und sey es so früh—
Mutterlieb, Herzchen, entschlummert doch nie.

Andantino Grazioso

Op. 5 No. 8

Carcassi is perhaps best known for his *Method, Op. 59*, and his *25 Melodic and Progressive Etudes, Op. 60*. Aside from these didactic works he published many collections of light-hearted pieces of moderate technical difficulty, a typical example being his *Op. 5, Le Nouveau Papillon*, from which the following two pieces are selected.

The original edition was quite fully fingered, and it has only been necessary to add some bar signs and to clarify ambiguous passages.

1. *The third finger should remain on the F♯ throughout the measure.*
2. *The slurs in this measure are editorial on the assumption that they were mistakenly omitted from the first edition.*

Suggested tempo is ♪ = 104.

Andantino Grazioso
Op. 5 No. 8

Matteo Carcassi
(1792-1853)

36

Allegretto

Op. 5 No. 12

1 *Note that once the second finger reaches the A on the second string the hand remains in position (9th) for the next three measures.*

2 *It may help to practise the broken thirds in this measure and the next as chords to clarify the left hand movements.*

3 *Original fingering for the high G was 3, here changed to 4 to release the third finger for the following A.*

Suggested tempo is ♩ = 66.

This plate taken from Carcassi's method illustrates the right hand position carried over from the lute, with the little finger resting on the soundboard near the bridge. Compare the freer right hand position shown in Aguado's method on page 4.

Allegretto

Op. 5 No. 12

Matteo Carcassi

Theme From Op. 102

Guitar arrangements of operatic solos were extremely popular in the early nineteenth century. This example is from the opera *Baccanali di Roma* by Generali, and is an arrangement of a Cavatina. It was first published by Diabelli, the complete work comprising *Introduction, Theme and Variations*, and also appeared as a quartet with guitar. The theme was reprinted in the English magazine for guitar enthusiasts *The Giulianiad* (1833-1835).

[1] *The hammer with the third finger is awkward, but it comes on a weak beat so there is no need to apply excessive force.*

Suggested tempo ♩ = 88.

Mauro Giuliani
(1781-1829)

Arietta

Op. 95 No. 3

Giuliani was celebrated as a singer as well as a guitarist, and frequently performed songs of his own composition. The original publication contained six *Ariette* dedicated to the Empress Marie-Louise who had shown considerable favor to Giuliani and had named him "honorary chamber virtuoso".

Portrait by Sir George Hayter, published in 1884.

Arietta
Op. 95 No. 3

Mauro Giuliani
Words by Metastasio

Quan - do sa - ra quel di, ch'io non ti senta in

sen sem - pre tre - mar co - si, po - ve - ro

co - re? po - ve - ro co - re?

Stel - le, che cru - del - ta! un sol pia - cer non v'é,

sem - pre tre - mar co - si, po - ve - ra co - re!

sem - pre tre - mar co - si, po - ve - ra co - -

re sem - pre tre - mar co - si po - ve - ro

co - re.

Caprice

Op. 20 No. 2

Legnani is perhaps best known as a close friend and associate of Paganini, with whom he gave a number of concerts. He was a prolific composer, with published works exceeding two hundred and fifty for solo guitar and small instrumental combinations, and he enjoyed a wide reputation as a virtuoso performer.

The *Caprice* is chosen from a series in all keys designed for technique development.

1. *In the original the B is slurred to the E—possible on the smaller fingerboard of the nineteenth century guitar, but here re-fingered for the modern instrument.*

2. *Although this passage may appear complicated, it is in fact simple as the same diminished chord is moved down through the various positions.*

Suggested tempo   ♩ = 76.

Luigi Legnani
(1790-1877)

45

Variations On A Favorite Theme For Two Guitars

Op. 57

Diabelli's compositions for two guitars are among his most successful works, those for solo guitar being largely directed to amateurs of limited technical ability.

The combination of first guitar with a capotasto on the third fret with second guitar at normal pitch was popular in the period, since it extended the range of the composition while giving each player essentially an easy part. As the duets are musically interesting and enjoyable to play they present a strong argument against the prejudice of some guitarists against the use of the capotasto in "classical" playing—a prejudice that was non-existent during the classical period.

After placing the capotasto on the third fret the first guitar simply reads the notes in the usual way, E being the top string open, F at the first fret after the capotasto, G at the third fret and so on. There is no need for mental transposition, as a few minutes experimentation will show.

[1] *Note that the low C# is not sustained, and the hand moves from the first to the second position when the first finger plays the high C#.*

[2] *This difficult movement is facilitated by leaving the third finger on the G# from the previous measure.*

[3] *The first finger slides are somewhat unusual, but are the composer's indications. The passage calls for practise until it is clearly understood.*

[4] *Note that both first and second fingers slide up for the change of position and that the second finger remains on the C in preparation for the following measure.*

Suggested tempo is ♩ = 66.

Variations On A Favorite Theme For Two Guitars Op. 57

Variation I

Variation II

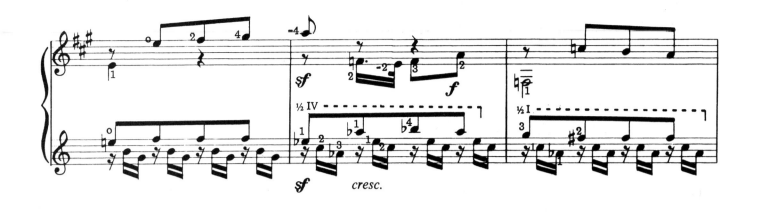

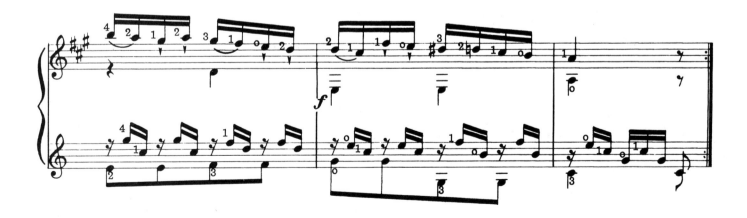

VARIATION III

VARIATION IV

Tempo di Marcia, Allegro

staccato *f*

pp

pp sempre

f

VARIATION V

Andantino Pastorale

Study In A

Op. 44 No. 20

Sor's *Opus 44* consisted of twenty-four little pieces of progressive difficulty "to serve as lessons for complete beginners." In common with other virtuosi, Sor somewhat over-estimated the capacity of the average complete beginner, but the pieces are attractive and melodic and not too technically demanding.

Perhaps more than all his contemporaries, Sor had the gift of writing instructional works with an intrinsic charm of their own which did not sound like didactic exercises. Unlike the more major works, these studies are extensively fingered by the composer.

1. *The slur applies to both notes. Only the D# and the B# are played by the right hand, and then the 2nd and 3rd fingers slide firmly up a fret to sound the E and C#.*

2. *The 2nd finger must stretch around the 3rd and 4th to find the F# —not difficult with practise.*

3. *The stretch between the 2nd and 4th fingers is considerable, and would have been easier on the smaller fingerboard of Sor's time. However it can be done, and serves as an exercise in extending the reach of the left hand.*

Suggested tempo is ♩ = 84.

Fernando Sor
(1778-1839)

Study In B Minor

Op. 31 No. 18

Opus 31 consisted of twenty-four progressive lessons for the guitar, "fingered with care, dedicated to beginning students."

This piece has the same melancholy beauty as the often played study in the same key, *Op. 35 No. 22*; but being less well-known presents a most attractive alternative to the standard work.

1. *The melody notes (stemmed upward) should be played* apoyando *(rest stroke) to bring them out above the accompaniment.*
2. *Note that the 4th finger remains to sustain the B throughout the sixteenth-note group.*
3. *Sor's fingering gives the 2nd finger on the B, here changed to 3rd as a misprint is assumed.*
4. *As above, the 2nd finger is changed to the 3rd.*

Suggested tempo is ♪ = 84.

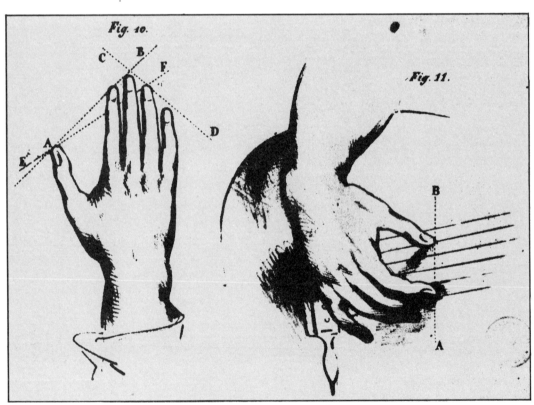

Hand positions from Sor's *Méthode.*

Study In B Minor
Op. 31 No. 18

Fernando Sor

Study In E

Op. 35 No. 8

Opus 35 was published in two parts, each containing a dozen short instructional pieces.
No. 8 is a typical light-hearted example of Sor's didactic writing.

[1] *The note values of the bass part are slightly unusual, since if the initial E is to last only a quarter-note one would expect an eight-note rest below the final beat. The implication is probably that both the E and the G♯ should be held for the remainder of the measure. The right hand fingering is editorial.*

[2] *Note that the two B's are sounded in unison on the open 2nd and 3rd strings.*

Suggested tempo is ♪ = 144.

Fernando Sor

Study In E Minor

Op. 35 No. 24

A note to the original edition of this study states, "The finger making the highest note should hold it until it is obliged to move to another." Essentially this is to simplify the notation, which otherwise would have to show the three voices thus:—

1. The suggestion for right hand fingering is editorial.
2. The original gives the third finger on the D, here changed to facilitate the move to the low C in the next measure.
3. The F♮ should sustain for the remainder of the measure according to Sor's note above.
4. Unfingered in the original, Sor would probably have avoided changing the direction of the arpeggio and fingered the passage thus:—

However on the modern fingerboard the stretch is too great; hence the simplification.

Suggested tempo is ♩ = 88.

Study In E Minor
Op. 35 No. 24

Fernando Sor

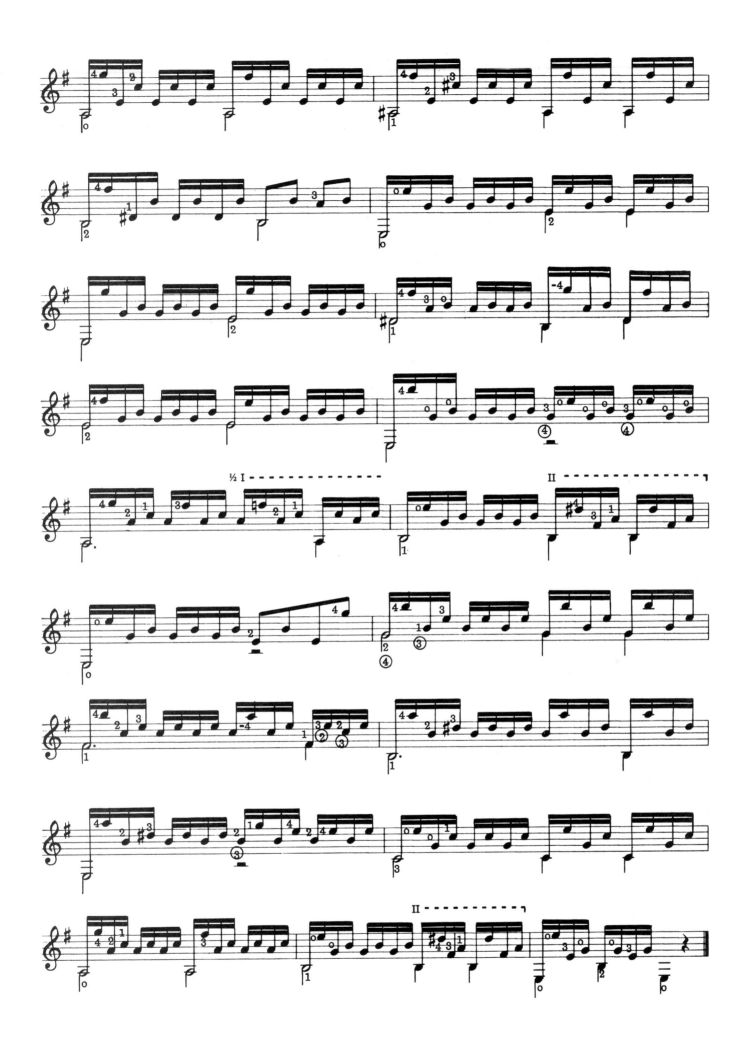

Study In E Minor

Op. 35 No. 18

Fully fingered by Sor, this attractive study should present few difficulties providing that
the left hand fingering is followed meticulously.
Suggested tempo is ♩ = 80.

Fernando Sor

Andantino

Study In E

Op. 44 No. 3

Although at first sight this study may appear more complex than the preceding ones, it is in fact of only moderate technical difficulty, and the greater rhythmic variety makes it an enjoyable piece to play.

The fingering is editorial, the original containing only very occasional indications.

1 *The right hand plays the G♯ and the B♯, then the left hand fingers slide firmly to sound the A and C♯.*

2 *This position is dictated by the quarter notes in the middle part. Care must be taken to select the correct strings with the right hand. The finger indications are from the original, this being the only passage that Sor felt it necessary to finger.*

Suggested tempo is ♪ = 88.

Study In E
Op. 42 No. 3

Fernando Sor

Study In E Minor

Op. 48 No. 5

Opus 48 consists of twenty-four studies of an advanced nature. *No. 5* is essentially an arpeggio study which uses the guitaristic device of moving chords around the inner strings while leaving the first string open to produce interesting combinations.

Once the left hand pattern is memorized, the piece is not hard to play since there is a logical and smooth series of movements through the various positions. It is effective and enjoyable to play.

The fingering, though editorial, is implicit in the score.

Suggested tempo is ♩ = 84.

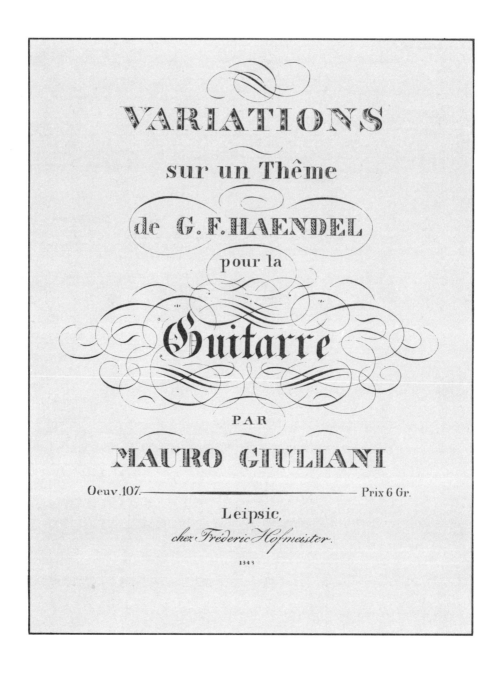

72

Study In E Minor
Op. 48 No. 5

Mauro Giuliani
(1781-1829)

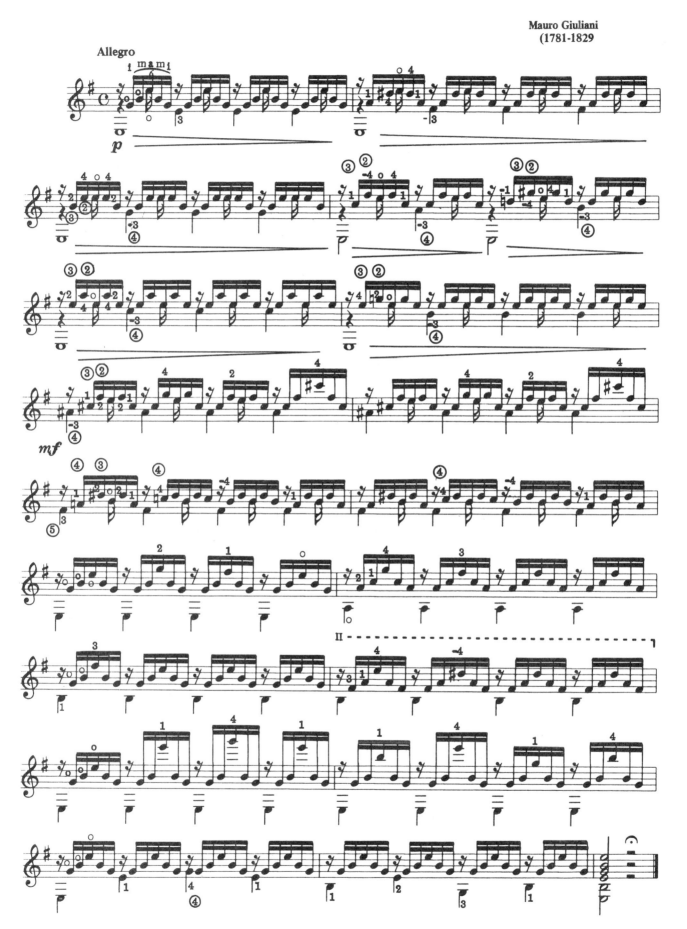

Le Premier Pas Vers Moi

Op. 53

The original edition of this duet bears the curious dedication "to those who, having learned to play this instrument, see the great difficulties for which correction is the only remedy." When taken in conjunction with the title, *The First Step Towards Me*, one must assume that Sor wished to encourage his students to work on their deficiencies as a first move toward the mastery that he possessed.

The original was fully fingered, and it has only been necessary to add an occasional clarification.

1. *This fingering is somewhat controversial at the present time; the alternative viewpoint would call for the use of the 3rd finger where the 2nd is used in this measure.*
2. *The notes indicate the string on which the natural harmonic is to be played, and the numbers indicate the fret. The 3rd fret harmonic is weak, but possible if the right hand plays close to the bridge.*
3. *The harmonic 9 is a correction of a 3 in the original—an error.*
4. *All but the first note of the group should be slurred together.*
5. *This passage is easy to play when the fingering is understood, and has a pleasant bell-like sound.*

Diagram from Sor's *Méthode* showing the little finger braced against the guitar as in Aguado's method.

Le Premier Pas Vers Moi
Op. 53

Fernando Sor

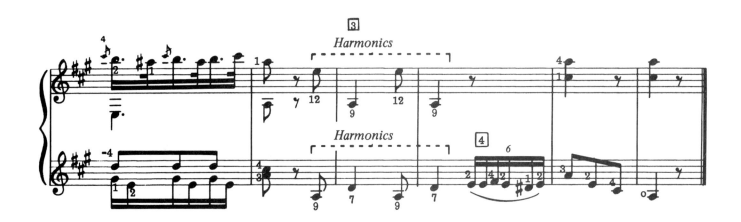

82

Study In E Minor

First published in 1820, this favorite study was reprinted in Aguado's instruction **method**. It presents some challenge, but is musically attractive and well worth the effort. **Aguado's** fingering indicates that he had a remarkable capacity to stretch the left hand, and **some of** his demands are impossible on the larger fingerboard of present times. **One such demand** has been simplified, as explained in note 2 below.

1. *This fingering is difficult, but comes with practise. With the 4th and 1st fingers in position the 3rd must be pushed into place.*
2. *Aguado fingered this measure with a bar at the third fret, considered virtually impossible on the modern guitar.*
3. *The second and fourth fingers must remain firmly on the D and G from the previous beat.*

Suggested tempo is ♩ = 69.

Study In E Minor

Study In A Minor

This study first appeared in Aguado's *Escuela de Guitarra* in 1825. It serves as an attractive performance piece as well as being an excellent exercise for the left hand. The sparse fingering of the original has been filled out for this edition.

[1] *Original:—*

[2] *In the original the bass C was a whole note—possible if this measure is taken in the eighth position, but I am more inclined to believe it an error.*

[3] *The jump of the 3rd finger from the A in the preceding measure to the bass G is extremely awkward, but there seems to be no logical alternative.*

[4] *The 4th finger move is from the original edition.*

[5] *In place of 2nd and 1st fingers the original gives 3rd and 2nd, assumed to be an error.*

[6] *Original:—*

[7] *The original gives the 3rd finger for the bass B♭.*

Suggested tempo is ♩ = 92.

Study In A Minor

Dionisio Aguado

Polonaise Concertante

Op. 137 No. 2

Opus 137, consisting of three *Polonesi Concertanti* in two movements was published by G. Ricordi of Milan some seven years after Giuliani's death. They were not fingered, but lie very naturally on the fingerboard and make few technical demands on the players.

[1] *The half bar is not strictly necessary but may help some players with this measure which requires special practise.*

[2] *It is important to bar the E♯ in preparation for the move to the second position bar in the next measure.*

Suggested tempo is ♩ = 72.

Allegretto

Mauro Giuliani
(1781-1829)

Trio

91

D. C., La Polonaise
al Fine

92

Minuet And Rondo From The Grand Sonata

Op. 22

Sor dedicated his *Grand Sonata* to the "Prince of Peace", a title given to Manuel Godoy, the powerful and controversial political figure elevated to prominence by Queen Maria Luisa of Spain. It has enjoyed considerable popularity over the years, in particular the final movements printed below.

The original was not fingered, so all suggestions are editorial.

1. *The sixteenth note group is sometimes played with a single slur; however, the original edition is quite specific in requiring two slurs throughout.*
2. *The cross-fingering may seem strange but works well at tempo.*
3. *A hard stretch, but there is no alternative that permits the bass quarter-notes to be sustained.*

93

Trio

Rondo

Allegretto

Andante Largo

Op. 5 No. 5

Sor's title to *Opus 5, Six Very Easy Little Pieces*, might be contested by those who perform the famous *Andante Largo* as a concert solo. It is a most effective piece, and if not "very easy" at least not very difficult.

There is only occasional fingering in the original.

1. *There is no fingering for the first line, so the positions are only a suggestion.*
2. *Although somewhat awkward this fingering is essential if the bass chord is to sustain for its full value.*
3. *The slurs are editorial, the original giving only the phrasing.*
4. *The only way to sustain the high A is to take it with the 2nd finger. If played with the 1st finger the note value must be "implied."*

5.

6. *There is no practical way to sustain the quarter-note F. On the smaller fingerboard of Sor's time it was probably taken with the 3rd finger.*

Suggested tempo ♪ = 66.

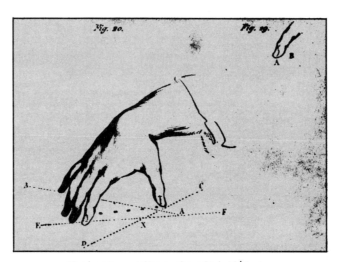

Hand movement diagram from Sor's *Méthode*.

Andante Largo
Op. 5 No. 5

Fernando Sor

99

Variations In Tremolo From Op. 21

Regondi achieved early fame as a child prodigy, and had performed in most European capitals by the age of nine. Sor composed a fantasy (*Souvenir D'Amitié Op. 46*) expressly for him, which may be taken as a considerable tribute to his ability.

His compositions are few, the one below being an extract from a lengthy *Theme and Variations*. It is interesting as one of the first examples of the use of tremolo technique in the nineteenth century.

The writing of the bass line is somewhat unusual, in that some of the notes overlap others forming, in effect, extra voices. As a practical solution, I suggest first playing the thumb part without the tremolo, taking care to give each note its correct value.

The fingering is editorial.

1. *The unusual fingering is necessary if the bass F is to sustain.*
2. *I would suggest placing the complete E chord at this point.*
3. *All three note chords should be played with p, i and m.*

Suggested tempo ♩ = 46.

Giulio Regondi in 1841; portrait by Viennese lithographer Josef Kriehuber.

Variations In Tremolo From Op. 21

Giulio Regondi
(1822-1872)

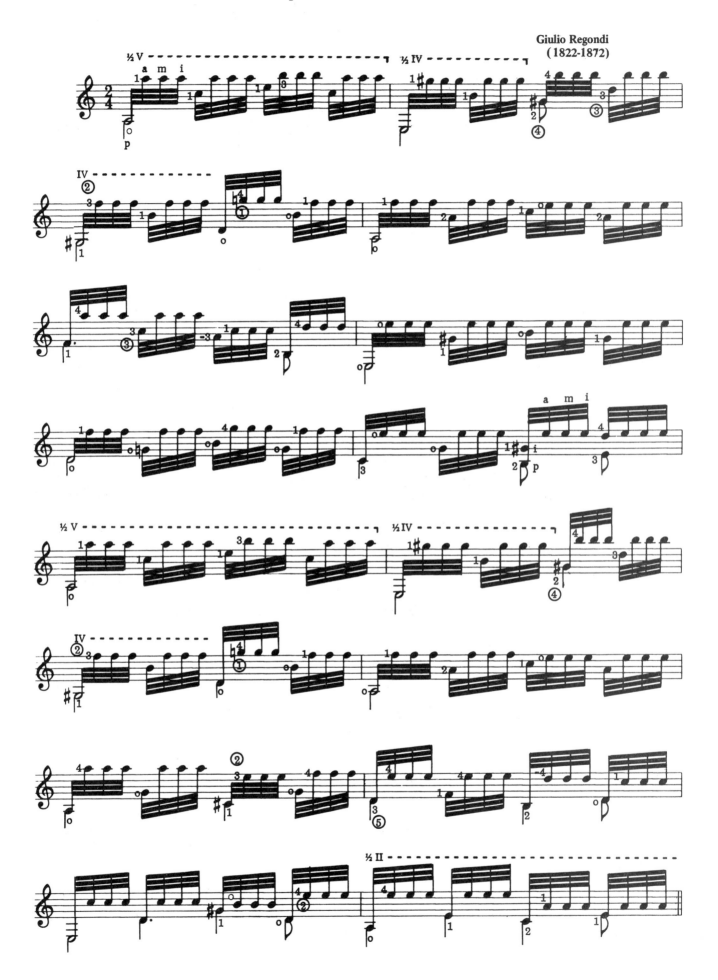

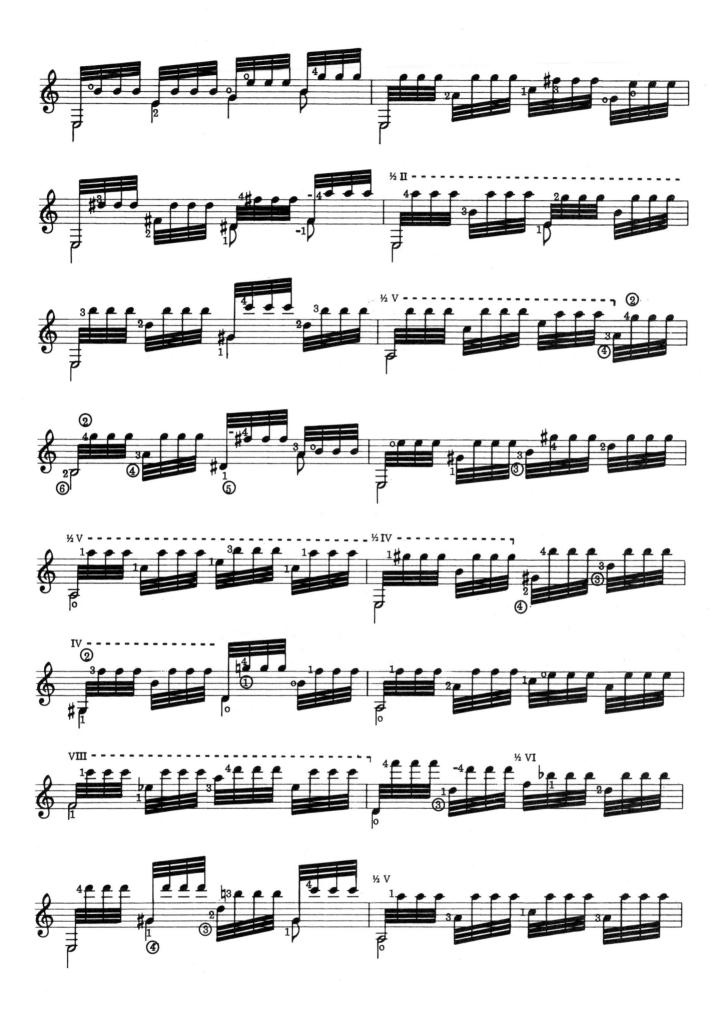

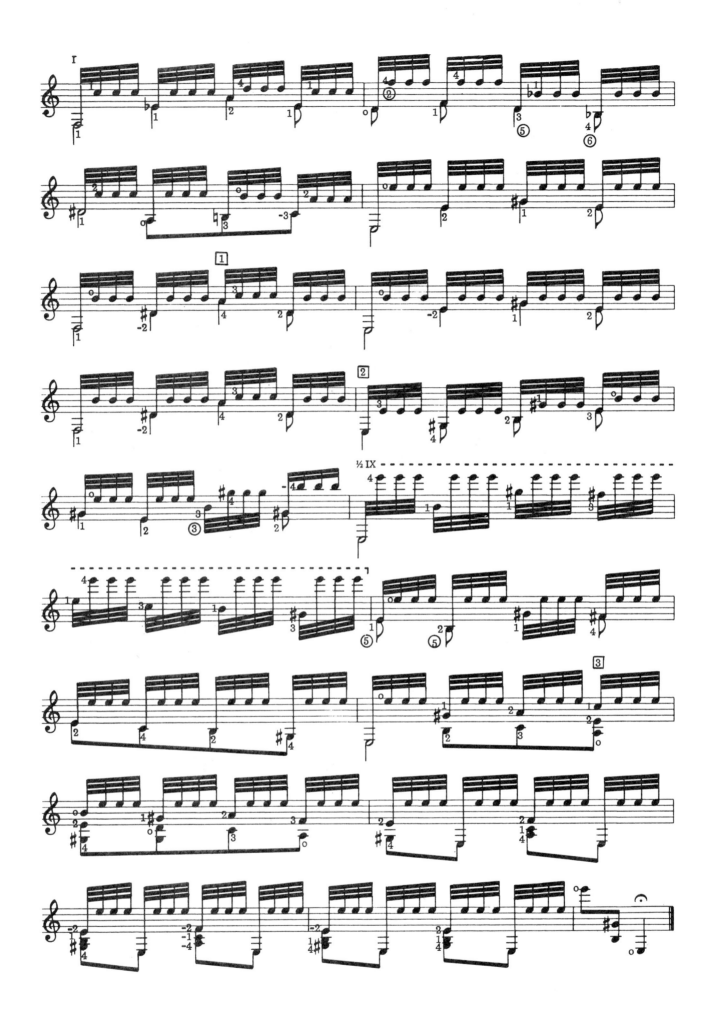

An Die Musik

Op. 88 No. 4

Although *An Die Musik* was not published with a guitar accompaniment as were so many of Schubert's songs, the structure of the piano part is so guitaristic that it is a pleasure to play this great favorite on the instrument with which it was probably originally conceived. (See Introduction p. 8).

Franz Schubert

An Die Musik
Op. 88 No. 4

Franz Schubert
(1797-1828)
Words by Fr. von Schober

Du hol - de Kunst, in wie - viel grau - en
Oft hat ein Seuf - zer, dei - ner Harf' ent -

Stun - den, wo mich des Le - bens wil - der
flos - sen, ein sü - sser, hei - li - ger Ac -

Kreis um - strickt, hast du mein
cord von dir, den Him - mel

106

Herz _____ zu war - mer Lieb' ent - zun - den, hast
bess' - rer Zei - ten mir er - schlos - sen, du

mich in ei - ne bess' - re Welt ent - rückt, in ei - ne
hol - de Kunst, ich dan - ke dir da - für, du hol - de

bess' - re Welt _____ ent - rückt!
Kunst, ich dan - ke dir!

Variations
On A Theme Of G. F. Handel
Op. 107

This famous Handel theme with accompanying variations was published in 1720 as the concluding movement of a suite. It became known as the *Harmonious Blacksmith*, though this title first appeared nearly a hundred years after the original publication, and its origin is still unknown.

The variations in this setting do not follow those of Handel and are Giuliani's own composition.

1. *In a number of places Giuliani appears to have written sustained notes which may not have been truly intended. In this case if the E is to sustain an alternative fingering would be:—*

2. *See note 1. To sustain the bass A would require over-complex fingering, which I feel was probably not the intention.*
3. *It is obviously impossible both to slur the bass A to the C♯ and to sustain it. I have given priority to the slur.*

Giuliani's tempo marking is ♩ = 88.

Mauro Giuliani
(1781-1829)

Variation I

Variation II

Variation III

(slargandosi)

a tempo

Variation IV

Variation V

Variation VI

Fantasy

Op. 7

A letter to the *Giulianiad* magazine (published 1833-35) defending Sor to a readership mainly of Giuliani fans cited this *Fantasy* as a demonstration of Sor's superior ability as a composer. It is certainly one of his most appealing works, beautifully recorded by Julian Bream. (RCA LSC-2878).

In the original, the largo is followed by a theme and variations. The fingering is editorial.

1. *The extended eighth position bar is tiring until the passage is memorized and played up to tempo.*
2. *The change of position is suggested in preparation for what follows.*
3. *An extreme stretch, but possible with practise.*
4. *For the trill I would suggest a simple Bb –C–Bb (i.e., a reverse mordent) with a similar treatment for those which follow.*

Suggested tempo ♪ = 76.

Fernando Sor
(1778-1839)

Variations
On La Folia And Minuet

Op. 15

The theme of *La Folia (Les Folies d'Espagne)* was a favorite one as the basis for variations from the 17th century onwards, and it was used by Corelli and Handel as well as the guitarists Robert de Visée and Gaspar Sanz.

Sor's version, *Opus 15*, was followed by a minuet in the major key possibly intended to be performed after the final variation and for this reason included here.

The fingering is editorial.

[1] *The slurred notes sounded simultaneously with plucked chords are unusual but do occur occasionally in the music of this period. Obviously the slur must be performed very clearly so that the second note has sufficient volume.*

[2] *In the original edition there were no slurs in the fourth variation. At times the decision to add slurs appears to have been left up to the player, and those included in this edition should be considered only suggestions.*

[3] *This is a problem passage, but if the bass notes are to sustain as written there is no alternative fingering.*

[4] *The fingering of the triplets is that of the composer.*

[5] *Slurs omitted in the original publication.*

Suggested tempo ♩ = 80.

A figure in the Minuet; from an engraving published in 1735 in Kellom Tomlinson's *The Art of Dancing*. Dance notation used in the Feuillet system appears on the floor.

Variations On La Folia And Minuet Op. 15

Fernando Sor

Variation II

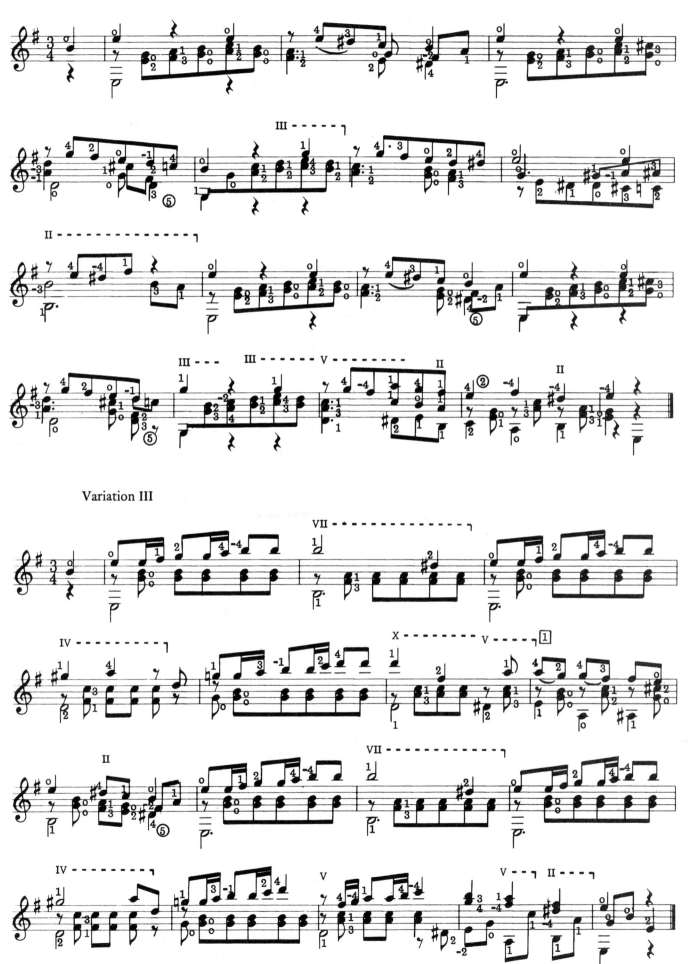

Variation III

119

Variation IV

Menuet

Andante

120

Grand Overture

Op. 61

The *Grand Overture* is one of Giuliani's most dramatic and brilliant compositions. A fine recording of the work is that of Julian Bream (RCA LSC-3070).

Although considerable technique is necessary to play the piece up to tempo, it is nevertheless very straightforward and idiomatic to the instrument and presents few unusual difficulties.

1 *The bass F♯ quarter-note in the original is impossible, and is here corrected to an eighth-note.*

2 *An alternative to this difficult change is:—*

3 *This passage could be taken on a fourth position bar, but done that way it is harder to eliminate the over-ring of the E chord when the D♯ is played.*

Suggested tempos, Andante sostenuto ♩ = 66, Allegro maestoso ♩ = 104.

Mauro Giuliani; engraving by Jügel based on the portrait by Stubenrauch.

Grand Overture
Op. 61

Mauro Giuliani

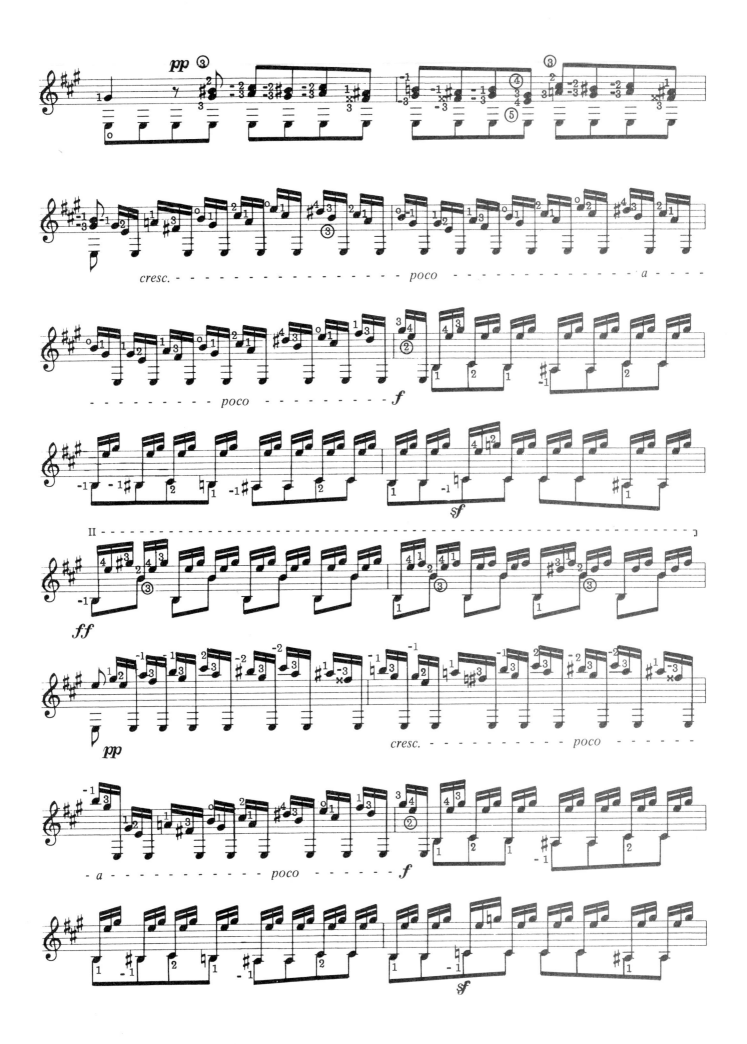

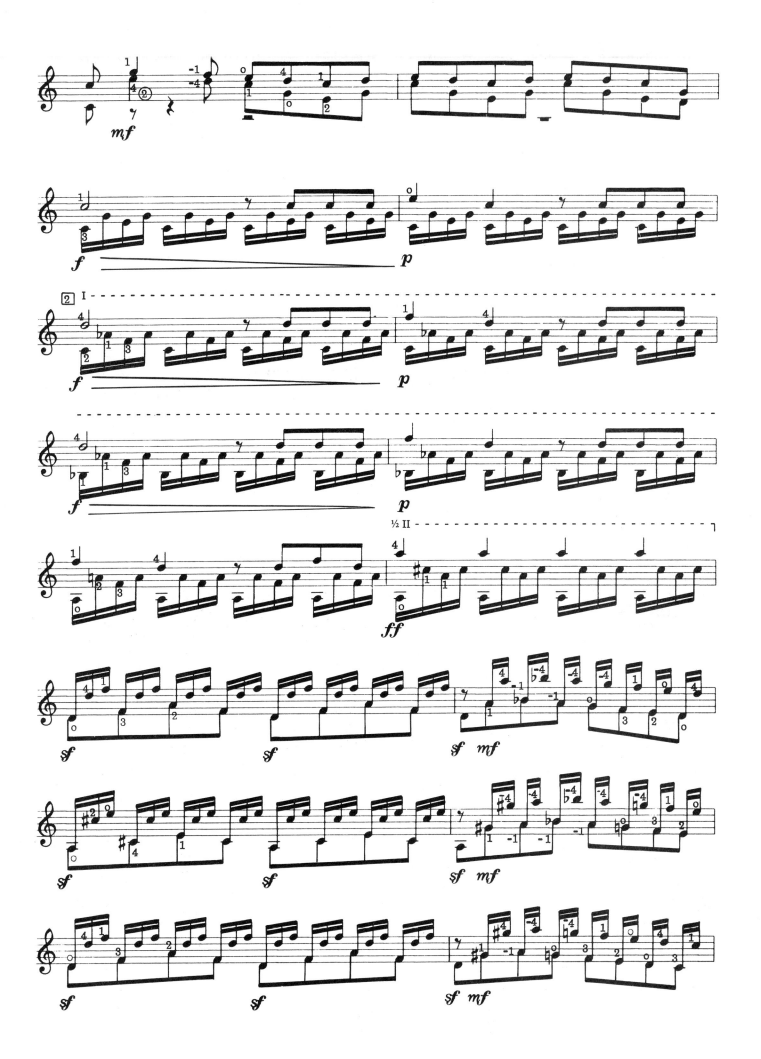

130

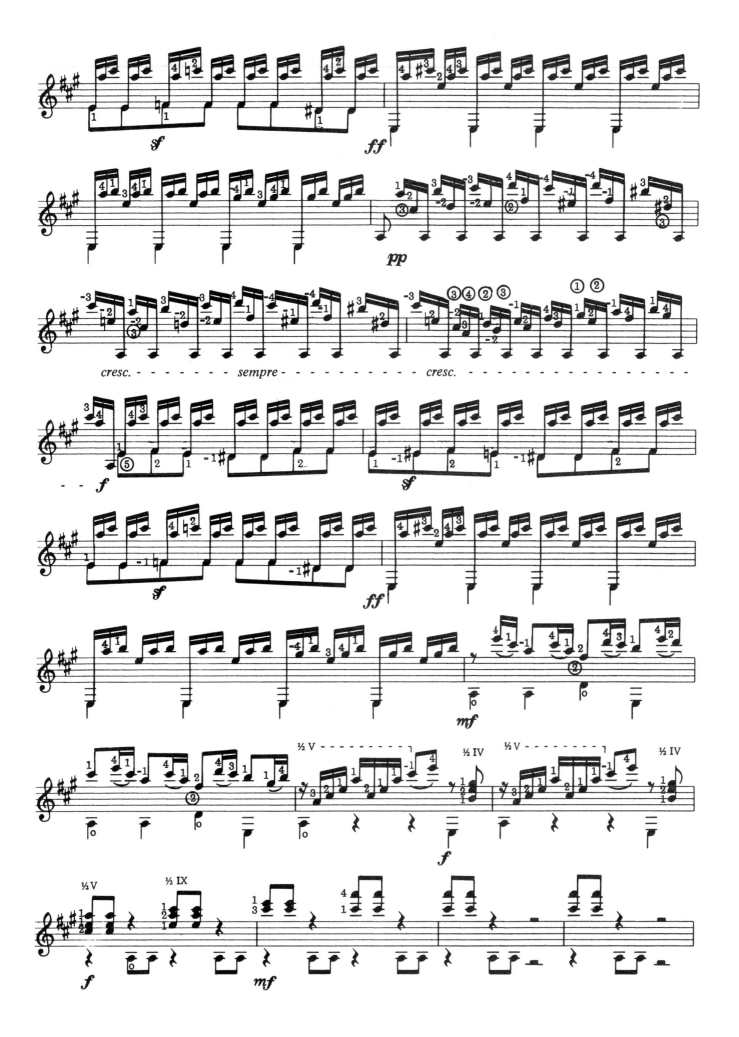

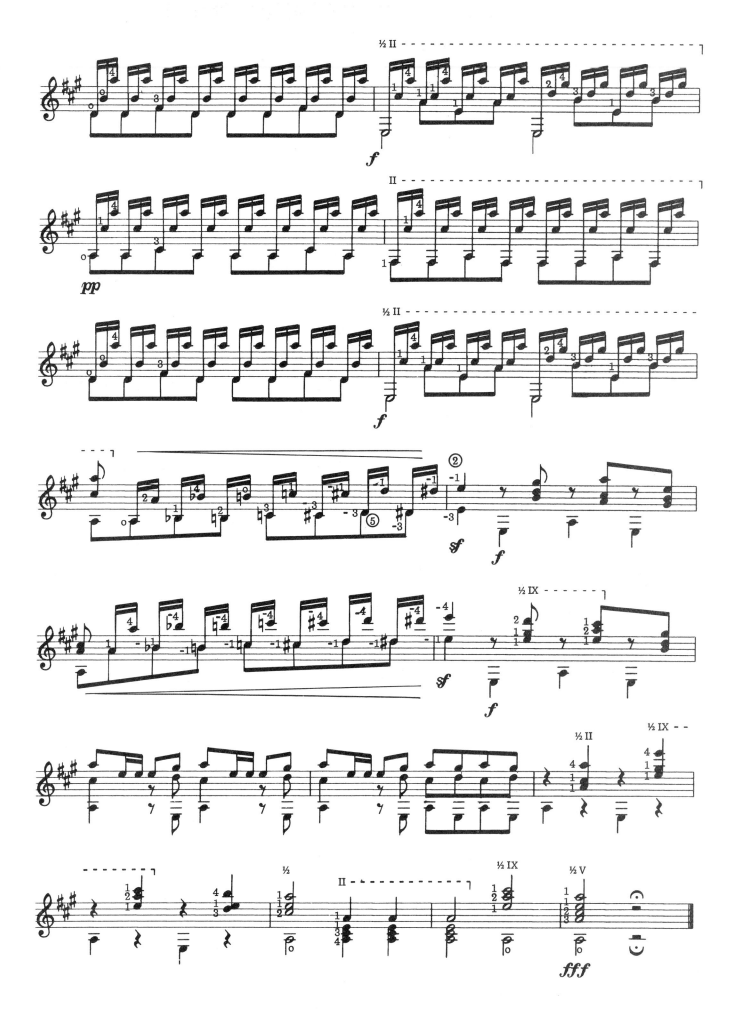

Grand Solo

Op. 14

This major work of Fernando Sor has suffered from a series of irresponsibly edited "revisions" in which chords have been radically changed or simplified, passages omitted, and other alterations made to suit the whim of the "reviser". In these circumstances it is hoped that the inclusion of this piece in its original form will help those who wish to play what the composer wrote rather than what some editor "feels" that he should have written.

The suggested fingerings are editorial.

|1|

|2| *Original:—*

|3| *In view of the staccato marking on the D, the sign here is presumably one of phrasing and not a slur.*

|4| *Players may wish to finger this passage another way to avoid the extreme stretch. However the slurring implies that it was done in this position, and overall it seems the most satisfactory.*

|5| *In spite of the extra note in the chord (low F♯) it may be assumed that the intention here is the same arpeggio that is spelled out eight bars ahead where the passage is repeated.*

|6| *A double slur: 3rd and 4th fingers both pull off to sound the A♯ and F♯.*

|7| *The 1st finger should be in bar position but with the tip raised so that the open D may sound.*

Suggested tempos, Introduction ♪ = 72, Allegro ♩ = 104.

Grand Solo
Op. 14

Introduction

Fernando Sor

138

smorz. poco a poco